Keeper of Accounts

Irena Klepfisz

PERSEPHONE PRESS, INC.
Watertown, Massachusetts

"Bashert" previously appeared in Sinister Wisdom 21; portions of "Bashert" appeared in Nice Jewish Girls: A Lesbian Anthology. "Contexts" previously appeared in Sinister Wisdom 17, Woman Poet: East, and Lesbian Poetry: An Anthology. "Glimpses of the Outside" previously appeared in Ikon 1 (1982). "Monkey I" previously appeared in Frontiers: A Journal of Women's Studies; "Monkey II" previously appeared in Conditions: One and Lesbian Poetry: An Anthology. "Work Sonnets" previously appeared in Conditions: Eight.

Cover design by Maria von Brincken.
Text design by Pat McGloin.
Typeset by Gloria Z. Greenfield.

First Edition. First Printing.

Library of Congress Cataloging in Publication Data

Main entry under title:

Keeper of accounts.

PS3561.L388K4   1982   811'.54   82-18910
ISBN 0-930436-17-2

For Judy Waterman

Acknowledgements

I am very grateful to my mother Rose Perczykow Klepfisz for volunteering financial support that enabled me for a period of time to focus entirely on my writing. In addition, I am indebted to Frances Hanckel, executor of Claudia Scott's estate, for other financial assistance made available through a provision of Claudia's will. As a result of their generosity, I was able to extend a planned writing period of three months into eight.

The eight months, when I was completely free from income-producing work, proved to be very productive. At the beginning of the summer of 1981, only the two "Monkey House" monologues (1976-77) and "Contexts" (1979) existed in completed form. The "Work Sonnets" were in rough draft (without the Notes or the Monologue) and the series "Urban Flowers" was only partially finished. Started well over a year and a half earlier, both were completed during this time. In addition, I began and finished "Glimpses of the Outside," "*Bashert*," and "A Poem for Judy/beginning a new job." Towards the end of this period, I began to think about another poem that ultimately emerged as "Solitary Acts"; but this took almost five months to complete because I had already returned to full-time work.

I feel it important to give this history of how *Keeper of Accounts* came to be written not only because I am grateful to my mother and Frances for making it possible, but also because I want to remind myself and others of the circumstances that are most conducive to creative work. A block of uninterrupted time—unencumbered by a job or financial anxiety—is critical to every form of creativity and rarely available to most of us, especially to those of us who are out of the mainstream. I feel particularly fortunate to have received it in these times of economic depression and do not want it to be taken for granted.

Irena Klepfisz
October, 1982

Contents

IV. Inhospitable Soil

Keeper of Accounts

I. From the Monkey House and Other Cages

From the Monkey House and Other Cages

The voices are those of female monkeys born and raised in a zoo.

Monkey I

/1/

from the beginning
she was always dry   though
she'd press me close
prying open my lips:

the water warm
the fruit   sour   brown
apples bruised and soft.

hungry for dark   i'd sit
and wait   devour dreams
of plain sun and sky
large leaves   trunks   dark
and wet with sweet thick sap.

        but morning
brought back the space
and cement   her weakened
body   my head against her
breast: my mouth empty.

yet she was   all
my comfort: her sharp
ribs against my cheek
her bony fingers   rough
in fluffing me dry.

she showed me   all
the space   the changing
colors outside   then

pulled me back   forced
me to sit with her
in a shadowy corner.

on certain clear days
she'd shrug   hold me in the sun:
her fur lacked smoothness
her body warmth.

in the midst of heat
they took me   with smooth
round strokes   and hushing
sounds.
      she sat silent
at first   sniffing their sweat
their stale breath   then leaped on one
her eyes wide   her claws poised and sharp.
      he grunted   deep
from within   an empty cavern
echoing the storm outside
flicked her off   and dragged me out.

i could hear her sound
as if a sea lion roared
then becoming tired
          drowned.

/4/

their space was smaller
cramped and low   the air
foul   with their sweat
their salt.
        and their motions
were sharp   as they spread me out
clamped me down
for the opening probe.

        i did not move
just sucked my breath
with each new venture   into my deepest parts
and then   with time
i became   a dark dull color
a gray rain   blending
with the liquid   of her eyes.

/5/

when they returned me
the air was ice:
bare branches   meshed
against a hard   dark sky.

i sat alone.   we were
separate now   though
she was still there
in the cage   next to mine.
her fur was stiff   her nostrils spread
she eyed me   circled
her back arched   ready for attack.

later   as the food was dropped
she leaped forward
hissed   snatched bits of fruit
from my side   of the bars.

/6/

a day   and a day
the pools   dead and dry
i'd sit and stare
into the cold   into the empty trees.

but she seemed   at rest
pressing against the bars
eyes closed   alone   on the other side.
only when i ate   she'd look sharp at me
her mouth moving
as i swallowed   each bite

and as night blackened us
she'd gather her scraps
enclose herself   in her arms.

the male   sleek-furred
was young   and active
when they forced him through to me.

i stayed in place   all
eyes and ready   while she leaped
in frenzy   retreated to the furthest wall.
he kept his distance
ignoring her   ignoring me
ate small morsels   tumbled
stared outside.

the ice was thawing
the pools filled and quiet.
i listened   as the soil
sopped   became mud
deep   and brown.

/8/

soon the trees budded   and i
pinked   softened   and presented.
he penetrated   withdrew
penetrated   withdrew
over   and over
till i was dry
and hard.
        she sat
relaxed and quiet
began to chew apples
slowly picking out
each black seed.

                    later
i cramped   shrivelled
then opened   wide   wide
my flesh thin and stretched
till: it burst forth
a thing   so strange
so pale   and hairless
a mass of flesh   separate from mine.

and through the heat
and heavy trees   the sound of water
the light of the moving sun:
the male ate regularly
the small one sucked
i mashed the sour fruit
between my lips.

she watched us all
as we would swallow
hoard   any piece of rind
or seed   that she could find.

the male was taken:
i turned my back.
the small one was taken:
i was held to one side.

and again   and again
the trees emptied again
the soil became hard
then became soft again.

and the cage is   all
mine   and i have myself:
touching my fur
pulling my face

while she moves so slowly
without any sound
eating   pacing
twisting her arms   around the hard bars.

/11/

sometimes at night   i watch
her asleep: the rigid bones
the thinned out fur

and i can see clearly
the sky   the bars
as we sat together
in a spot of sun
and she   eyes closed
moved me
moved me
to the sound of the waters
lapping
in the small   stone pools
outside.

Monkey II

/1/

to state each horror
would be redundant.   the objects
themselves suffice: a broken comb
an umbrella handle   a piece of blue
plastic   chipped pocket mirror.

the face is unfriendly.
i try to outstare it   but
it persists   moving

spastically   the eyes
twitching   open   shut
nose quivering   wrinkled fingers
picking at the ears.   i do not know

this stranger.

/2/

i have heard of tortures
yet remain
strangely safe.

                but at night
i am torn by my own
dreams   see myself live
the grossest indignities   probes

and unable to rip myself from my flesh
i remain silent   not
uttering sound   nor moan   not
bothering to feel pain.

waking   in early light
alone   untouched
i cry over my safety.

when they first come
they screech with wildness
flinging themselves against the wall
and then against the bars.

some sit and cry for days
some   never recover and
die.
        they are familiar
yet crap uncontrollably   plead
shiver and rock.   i refuse

to have anything to do with them
till they learn to behave.

/4/

at her arrival   she was
stunned and bruised.   she
folded up   refusing to eat

her mouth grim.   i staked
out my territory   recognizing
her fierceness   her strength.

but she weakened   grew sick
was removed without resistance
returned three days later
shaved patches on her arms.

later she told me: we create
the responses around us.

/5/

i remember the grasp of her claws
the vicious bite   the scar
still on my leg.   she was crazed

jabbering   then attacking
again.   and the sun seemed to fall away
into coldness   as i pressed myself
against the corner   the hardened sand
under my nails.   i began to gnaw
through concrete   my face raw.

they took her away
and when she came back
she did not look at me.

scatter yourself
i told her   moving
myself into the left
corner   where i sat
observing the movement
of her head.

                  she nodded
seemed to sleep
then stood up   pointing
outside.   the leaves were
red.   it was a falling time
noisy   dry twigs cracking
off nearby trees.   i felt

content   watching myself
while she pointed   the leaves
red.

                    and finally
she said   this is enough
and began to bang her head
against the wall   one thud

after another thud   she batted
herself beginning to bleed
throwing herself and falling.

they came   and tried to seize
her   while the sun vanished
and the trees   moved slowly

and everyone   so still
afraid to breathe: the moon
all fresh   and the birds
small balls of feathers.

i puked as they dragged her out:
tufts of fur on the stone floor.

/8/

when she died   i mourned
a silent mourning.
                    and
the others asked
asked   asked
and poked at me.

there had been much between us
in gesture.   mostly i remember
her yellowed teeth   her attempt
at tameness.

there had been no sound:
just the motion of   our hands
our lips sucked in
toes pointed   outward.
it had been enough.

                              dizzy
with messages   i would lie
down   dream of different
enclosures.

II. Different Enclosures

Contexts

for Tillie Olsen

> "Dollars damn me."
> —Herman Melville, as cited in *Silences*

> "I have no patience with this dreadful idea that whatever you have in you has to come out, that you can't suppress true talent. People can be destroyed; they can be bent, distorted, and completely crippled."
> —Katherine Anne Porter, *ibid.*

I.

I am helping proofread the history
of a dead language. I read out loud
to an old man whose eyes have failed
him. He no longer sees the difference
between a period or a comma, a dash
or a hyphen, and needs me for I under-
stand how important these distinctions are.

The room is crammed with books, books
he had systematically tagged for future
projects—now lost. Sounds pour out
of me. I try to inject some feeling
and focus, concentrate on the meaning
of each linguistic phrase. On the edge
of my vision, he huddles over a blurred
page, moves his magnifying glass from line
to line, and we progress. Time passes.
My voice is a stranger's, sensible and
calm, and I, the cornered, attentive hostess,
listen in silence as it conjectures the his-
tory of languages long dead without a trace.
How, I wonder, did I become what I am not?

I request a break. The sounds cease.
I check the clock, calculate, write
figures in a notebook. I am numb
and stiff, walk up and down the hall,
stare into busy offices. I wait.

I wait for something forgotten, something
caught and bruised: a brown feather,
a shaft of green light, a certain word.
I bend, drink water, remember stubborn
clams clinging to the muddy bottom.

II.

The building across the street
has an ordinary facade, a view of the park
and rows of symmetrical spotless windows.
Each morning, the working women come to perform
their duties. They are in starched white,
could pass for vigilant nurses keeping
order and quiet around those about to die.
And each morning, idle women
in pale blue housecoats, frilled and fluffed
at the edges, stare out of double windows,
waiting for something to begin.

With whom would you change places, I ask
myself, the maid or the mistress?

III.

The clock sucks me back. I calculate the loss,
return to the books, his unrecognizing eyes.
He is unaware of the pantomime outside,
feels no rage that I and the world are lost
to him, only mourns the words dead on the page.
We begin again. I point to the paragraph,
synchronize the movement of eye and mouth,
abandon all pretense of feeling. Silently I float
out, out toward the horizon, out toward the open sea,
leaving behind the dull drone of an efficient machine.

I am
there again, standing by the railing, watching
the whales in their narrow aquarium, watching
their gleaming grace in the monotonous circle, watching
how they hunger for fleshly contact, how the young keeper
places his human hand in their rough pink mouths,
rubs their tongues, splashes them like babies. I cannot
watch them enough, but feel deeply ashamed for I know
the price.

With a shock I realize we are not together,
that he is lost, caught in a trap.
He sounds the words over and over, moves
the glass back and forth, insists there is
a lapse in meaning. I sit silent, tense, watch
as he painfully untangles the subtle error, watch
as he leans back exhausted saying: "I knew something
was wrong! I knew from the context that something
was wrong!"

IV.

At the end of the day I stack the galleys,
mark an *x* where we've been forced to stop.
He is reluctant to let me go, anxious, un-
certain about the coming days, but I smile,
assure him they'll be all the same. Alone,
I rush for the bulb-lit train, for the empty
corner of the dingy car, then begin the struggle
against his vacant stare, against the memory
of the crowded shelves.

It is a story, I tell myself, at least
a story, that one Sunday when I refused
to go to work. Fifteen, bored with inventory
and weekend jobs, I stayed in bed and,
already expert, called in sick. Her rage
was almost savage, wild. She paced
through the apartment, returned to me again
and again saying *"Get up! Get up now!"*
as if I were in mortal danger. But nothing
would move me from my bed, from the sun
cutting through the iron fire escape outside,
from the half-finished book about the man
and the whale. "It's not that much money,"
I called to her.

And then her inexplicable silence. At first
she sat in the kitchen, fingering the piece
of cloth, staring absently at the teacup.
Finally she got up, began pinning the pattern.
Soon I heard the clean sound of the scissor
against the kitchen table, then silence again
as she basted. Much later that day, she worked
on the machine, and still she did not speak
to me, just let the bobbing needle make its own
uninterrupted noise. And as I went to bed
new with the excitement of that sea of words,
filled with my own infinite possibilities, she
continued sewing, fulfilling her obligation
for the next day's fitting.

V.

The blind man balances easily in the rocking
car. He moves among us, sings, shakes a tin
cup. Most of us think it's all a con, but it
makes no difference. Pose is part of necessity.
Riding each evening through the echoing tunnels,
I've begun to believe in the existence of my own
soul, its frailty, its ability to grow narrow,
small. I've begun to understand what it means
to be born mute, to be born without hope of speech.

Work Sonnets
with Notes and a Monologue

I: Work Sonnets

i.

iceberg
I dream   yearning
to be fluid.
through how many nights
must it float   cumbersome
for how many centuries
of sun   how many
thousands of years
must it wait
so that one morning
I'll wake
as water of lake
of ocean
of the drinking well?

and day breaks.

ii.

today was another day. first i typed some
letters that had to get out. then i spent
hours xeroxing page after page after page
till it seemed that i was part of the machine
or that it was a living thing like me. its
blinking lights   its opening mouth   looked
as if they belonged to some kind of terrible
unthinking beast to whom i would always be bound.
oblivious to my existence   it simply waited
for its due   waited for me to keep it going
waited for me to provide page after page after page.
when it overheated   i had to stop while it
readied itself to receive again. so i typed
some letters that had to get out. and he said

he was pleased with the way things were going.

iii.

today was my day for feeling bitter. the xerox
broke down completely   and the receptionist
put her foot down   and made it clear to the repairmen
that *we* couldn't afford to keep such a machine
and it was costing *us* extra money everytime *we* had
to xerox outside. they hemmed and hawed and said
the fuzz from the carpet clogged things up   and
then they worked on it. and she watched over them
and made sure it was going properly when they left.
by then i'd fallen behind and he asked me to stay
late   and i said i was tired and really wanted to go
home. so he said it was really important and i could
come in late tomorrow with pay. so i said okay and
stayed. but i didn't feel any better about it.

a morning is not an evening.

iv.

volcano
I dream   yearning
to explode.
for how many centuries
of earth   relentless
grinding   how many
thousands of unchanged
years   buried
will it take
so that one morning
I'll wake
as unfettered flame
as liquid rock
as fertile ash?

and day breaks.

v.

today was my day for taking things in stride.
i was helpful to the temp in the office next
door   who seemed bewildered and who had definitely
lied about her skills. the dictaphone was
a mystery to her and she did not know how to use
the self-erasing IBM nor the special squeezer
to squeeze in words. she was the artist type:
hair all over the place   and dirty fingernails.
i explained everything to her   during her coffee
break   when she had deep creases in her forehead.
i felt on top of things. during lunch
i went out and walked around window shopping
feeling nice in the afternoon sun. and then
i returned and crashed through a whole bunch

of letters so i wouldn't have to stay late.

vi.

today was my day for feeling envy. i envied
every person who did not have to do what i
had to do. i envied every person who was rich
or even had 25 cents more than me   or worked
even one hour less. i envied every person who
had a different job   even though i didn't want
any of them either. i envied poor homeless children
wandering the streets because they were little
and didn't know the difference   or so i told myself.
and i envied the receptionist who'd been there
for years and years and years and is going to retire
soon   her hearing impaired from the headpiece she'd
once been forced to wear. For her it was over.
She was getting out. i envied her so much today.

i wanted to be old.

vii.

rock
I dream   yearning
to yield.
how many centuries
of water pounding
for how many thousands
of years   will it take
to erode this hardness
so that one morning
I'll wake
as soil
as moist clay
as pleasure sand
along the ocean's edge?

and day breaks.

viii.

today we had a party. he said he had gotten a
new title and brought in a bottle of wine during
lunch and we all sat around and joked about how
we'd become such important people and drank the
wine. and the receptionist got a little giddy
and they told her to watch it or she would develop
a terrible reputation which was not appropriate for
someone her age and maturity. and she laughed and
said "that's all right. i'll risk it." and the temp
from the office next door came in to ask me to go to
lunch. so we gave her some wine and she said she'd
been hired permanently and was real happy because
she'd been strung out and getting pretty desperate.
i noticed her hair was tied back and her nails neater.

and then we all got high and he said to everyone
this was a hell of a place. and then he announced
he had a surprise for me. he said he was going to
get a new xerox because it was a waste of my time to
be doing that kind of work and he had more important
things for me to do. and everyone applauded and the
receptionist said she hoped this one was better than
the last because we sure were losing money on that
old clinker. and he assured her it was. and then he
welcomed the temp to the floor and said "welcome aboard."
and he told her across the hall they treat their people
like we treat our people and their place is one hell
of a place to work in as she'd soon discover. and then
he winked over in my direction and said: "ask her.

she knows all about it."

ix.

dust
I dream   yearning
to form.
through how much emptiness
must it speed
for how many centuries
of aimless orbits
how many thousands
of light years   must it wait
so that one morning
I'll wake
as cratered moon
as sea-drenched planet
as exploding sun?

and day breaks.

and day breaks.

Says she's been doing this for 12 years. Her fifth job since she started working at 18. The others were: office of paperbox manufacturing co. (cold and damp almost all year round); office of dress factory (was told she could also model for buyers; quit because buyers wanted to feel the materials and her; was refused a reference); office of make-up distributor (got discounts on products); real estate office; and this, which she considers the best one. Through high school, she worked part-time contributing towards household expenses.

Extremely sharp with them. Says: "I'm not a tape recorder. Go through that list again." Or: "It's impossible. I've got too much to do." Two days ago, she told me: "Make *them* set the priorities. Don't make yourself nuts. You're not a machine."

Am surprised, because I always feel intimidated. But she seems instinctively to understand power struggles. Is able to walk the fine line between doing her job well and not knocking herself out beyond what she thinks she is being paid for. And she *is* good. Quick. Extremely accurate. Am always embarrassed when they return things with errors and ask me to do them over again. Never happens to her. She's almost always letter perfect.

I've told her she should demand more. The dictaphone is old and the typewriter is always breaking down. She should make them get her better equipment. It's too frustrating the way it is. She shrugged. Said it really didn't matter to her. Was surprised at her indifference.

Friendly, yet somehow distant. Sometimes I think she's suspicious of me, though I've tried to play down my background. I've said to her: "What's the difference? We're doing exactly the same work, aren't we?" Did not respond. Yet, whenever I've had trouble, she's always been ready to help.

Her inner life: an enigma. Have no idea what preoccupies her. Would be interested in knowing her dreams. Hard for me to imagine. This is a real problem. 1st person demands such inside knowledge, seems really risky. Am unclear what the overall view would be. What kind of vision presented. How she sees the world. How she sees herself in it. It seems all so limited, so narrow. 3rd person opens it up. But it would be too distanced, I think. I want to be inside her. Make the reader feel what she feels. A real dilemma. I feel so outside.

Says she reads, but is never specific what. Likes music, dancing. Smokes. Parties a lot, I think, for she seems tired in the morning and frequently says she did not get much sleep. Lives by herself. Thinks she should get married, but somehow can't bring herself to do it. "I like having the place to myself," she said the other day. Didn't specify what she was protecting.

Attitude towards them remains also unformulated. Never theorizes or distances herself from her experience. She simply responds to the immediate situation. Won't hear of organizing which she considers irrelevant (and also foreign inspired). Yet she's very, very fair and helpful to others and always indignant if someone is being treated unfairly. Whenever a temp arrives, she always shows her what's what. Tells her not to knock herself out. Reminds her to take her coffee break. Once gave up her lunch hour so one of them could go to the dentist for a bad tooth. Did it without hesitation. For a stranger.

Q: Is she unique or representative? The final piece: an individual voice? or a collective one?

I've learned a lot here, I think. It hasn't been as much of a loss as I expected. At least I've gotten some ideas and some material. But thank god I'm leaving next week. Can't imagine spending a whole life doing this.

III: A Monologue about a Dialogue

And she kept saying: "There's more. Believe me, there's more."

And I was kind of surprised because I couldn't imagine what more there could be. And then I began to wonder what she meant by the more, like maybe a bigger apartment or more expensive restaurants.

But she said that wasn't it, not really. "I'm not materialistic," she said and then looked kind of hopeless, as if I could never understand her. "I just want to *do* something," she said, obviously frustrated. And she looked hopeless again. And then she took a big breath, as if she was going to make a real effort at explaining it to me.

"It's just," she said, "it makes no difference whether I'm here or not. *Anyone* can do this. And I've always wanted to do special, important work."

Well, that made me laugh, because I've stopped wanting to do any work at all. All work is bullshit. Everyone knows that. No matter how many telephones and extensions, no matter how many secretaries, no matter how many names in the rolodex. It's all bullshit.

But she disagreed. "No," she said. "There's really important work to be done."

"Like what?" I asked curious, for I've seen enough of these types running around telling me how important it is to do this or that and just because they're telling me it's important they start feeling that they're important and doing important work. So I was curious to see what she'd come up with.

But she was kind of vague, and said something about telling the truth and saying things other people refused to say. And I confess I'd never heard it put that way before.

"I want to be able to say things, to use words," she explained.

"Oh, a writer," I said. I suddenly understood.

"Well, yes. But not like you think. Not romances or anything like that. I want to write about you and how you work and how it should be better for you."

"So that's it," I said, understanding now even more than I had realized at first. "So that's the important work. That certainly sounds good. Good for you, that is. But what about me? Do you think there's more for me? Because I'm not about to become a writer. And I don't know why I should just keep doing this so you have something to write about that's important. So can you think of something more for me? I mean I can't do anything except this."

And I could feel myself getting really mad because I remembered how in school they kept saying: "Stop daydreaming and concentrate!" And they said that your fingertips had to memorize the letters so that it would feel as if they were part of the machine. And at first it seemed so strange, because everything was pulling me away, away from the machine. And I really wanted to think about what was going on outside. There seemed so many things, though I can't recall them now. But they kept pushing me and pushing me: "Stop daydreaming! Concentrate!" And finally I did. And after a while it didn't seem so hard to do. And I won first prize in class. And the teacher said I'd have a real good choice in the jobs I could get because quality is always appreciated in this world and with quality you can get by.

And when I remembered how I'd sat doing those exercises, making my fingertips memorize the letters, I was real mad because she was no different than the others. There's always something more. More for them. But not one notion about something more for me. Except maybe a better machine so that I can do more work more quickly. Or maybe a couple of hours less a week. That's the most that they can ever think of for me.

And I was so furious. I'd heard all this before. And I know that as soon as they tell you they'll fight to get you better working conditions, they go home and announce: "You couldn't pay me enough to do that kind of work." That's what they say behind your back.

And I started to yell at her: "If you got words and know what to say, how come you can't come up with something more for me?"

And she was so startled. I could see it in her eyes. I mean you've got to have nerve. I'm supposed to just stay here while she writes about me and my work.

And then I said: "They're always going to need people to type the final copies. And I can see you'll never waste your time with that once you've thought of all the right words." And she kind of backed up, because I must have looked really mad. And she bumped into the file cabinet and couldn't move back any further. And I said to her: "What's the difference to me? It's all the same. I always end up doing the same thing. So let's make it clear between us. Whenever you finish whatever it is you're writing about me and my work, don't count on me to help you out in the final stages. Never count on me, no matter how good the working conditions."

A Poem for Judy
beginning a new job

I will keep this simple
not give it
universal significance
nor transform it
into art.

You say:
"I will not do this
forever. I *will* paint."

I've learned now
that it's no solace
to point out   the others
so many others
straining   wasting
unable to do
what they know
they must do

for such loss
is always solitary
and unshared
outside the scope
of bloodless theory.

You do not paint
and what must happen
does not happen:
the transformation
on the empty canvas
of the elusive marble
into the shadowy water
or of the simple water
into impenetrable rock

and nothing
nothing
not even a loving embrace
nor special intimate
midnight talk
will ever make up

or diminish that loss
for you
or for her
or her
or her

or her.

III. Urban Flowers

Mnemonic Devices:
Brooklyn Botanic Gardens, 1981

1.

I'd forgotten. Despite the planters
blossoming in the northern light
despite the potted succulents
over which you take such care
and patience   despite the window boxes
wired to the crumbling ledges
I'd forgotten.

This morning   at the pond's edge   we watch
the energetic ducks   chase and fly
in enigmatic patterns. I declare it
a mating dance—an educated guess—
having lost the thread of cycles
seasons   time   except when April's
sharp insistent air   distracts us
from this city's bitter dream
and we rise one morning   and remember:

there are still the gardens.

2.

It is a ritual   for us
this annual return
to the unsuppressed spring
in this guarded landscape
to the flowers   and trees
earth   rocks   pond.

It is the stuff of mythology
both old and new   as we relive
once more   a certain day
suddenly grown   strange
and dim   and how we stood
uncertain and afraid
of the exploding lightning
and the silent trees.

That day   awakened in us images
long lost   amid the dangers
of the city streets   and
we stood amazed   at the sight
and sound   wondering
what else   we'd lost.

That day   the gardens
drenched in violent rains
were transformed   into a raw
uncultivated place. And we
were   wearied wanderers
dazed   in awe   having suddenly
stumbled into our native land.

Royal Pearl

Where do new varieties come from?
General Eisenhower is a red tulip which was first recognized in 1951.

In 1957 a lemon yellow mutation appeared in a field of red General Eisenhower tulips. This yellow mutation proved to be a stable sport which was called—Royal Pearl.
—Brooklyn Botanic Gardens

In dead of winter   imprisoned within
the imprisoned earth   it was a leap
defiant   of all eternal laws   and patterns.
Beneath the frozen earth   it came to be
like a splitting of an inner will
a wrenching from a designated path
a sudden burst   from a cause unknown.
And then in spring   it opened: a lemon yellow
in a pure red field.

Our words deny the simple beauty
the wild energy of the event. *Anomaly*
deviant   mutant   we're always taught
as though this world   were a finished place
and we the dull guardians   of its perfected forms.
Our lives are rooted in such words.

Yet each winter   there are some
who watch   the gardens   emptied
only white   as the snow presses
on the fenced-in grounds   just
as on an unclaimed field.
And each winter   there are some
who dream   of a splitting of an inner will
a wrenching from the designated path
who dream a purple flower   standing solitary
in a yellow field.

Lithops

Common name: living stone

Barely differentiated
from the inorganic   they conceal
their passions   in sheer survival.
It is philosophy: life's hard
growth and erosion   even rocks
in the end   are broken down
to formless dust.

But like all schema   incomplete
for between the grey and fleshy
crevices   strange blossoms grow
in brazen colors. For us it is
the ancient sign   that every life
has its secret longings   to transcend
the daily pressing need
longings   that one day   must flower.

Aesthetics

No beauty for beauty's sake here.
Life's too lean
a constant   "Let's get down
to brass tacks." Function and necessity.
Stone and water.

Like the popularity of narcissus bulbs
this season. Not as you'd expect
for the plant itself   which sprouts
endless green stalks   that rise up
stiff and straight   and then finally
eke out a few buds of puny white flowers.
Nor for the obvious lesson by example:
the unavoidable six weeks (maybe more)
of patient preparation   before
any real prospects of blooming.

But rather   for the roots beneath.
Brown tipped and firm   they probe
and press around the artificial stones
in intricate networks   even dead-end mazes
daring anyone to trace them back
to their original source. In the stores
the saleswomen warn: "They can toss
the stones right out of the container!"
And here   that remains the real attraction.

Winter Light

Almost December. Indifferent
to seasons   the marigolds
persist. I am surprised by their pluck
and lack of propriety
their ability to ignore
the inappropriate:
a rusted leaking window box
a shaky fire escape
leading to a cemented street
below. They do not mourn
that all good things must
come to an end   and accept
that end as fate or destiny.
Instead   without struggle
or assessment of soil
moisture   heat   air   they continue
blooming   in chilling winter light
exactly as they did all summer.

Oleander

A gift from a lover when things
were definitely   going downhill.
"It's poisonous," she said.
"No known antidotes."
After the breakup   long after
when I'd already settled down
with someone else   I boarded it
with my mother   who's always taught:
never throw anything out.

Whenever I see it   I am drawn again
to the sembling innocence   among the dark
green jade and purple passion. I long
to taste one leaf   one petal   to test
that warning   for nothing   I tell myself
not even death   could be that final.
You must understand   it is more
than mortal resistance
for there was a time   when she left
and I knew   was fiercely certain
this departure   was the last.

Cactus

for my mother
Rose Perczykow Klepfisz

The pot itself was half the story.
A yellow ceramic dime store knickknack
of a featureless Mexican
with a large sombrero   pushing a wagon
filled with dirt.

The cactus was the other half.
Self-effacing   it didn't demand much
which was just as well
since she had no spare time
for delicate cultivation.
Used to just the bare essentials
it stood on our kitchen windowsill
two floors above the inhospitable soil
and neither flourished   grew
nor died.

I'd catch her eyeing it
as she stood   breathless
broiling our dinner's minute steaks
her profile centered in the windowframe.
She understood   the meaning   of both pot
and plant   still would insist there was
something extra   the colors yellow
green   or as she once explained
in her stiff   night school English:
"It is always   of importance to see
the things aesthetical."

Abutilon in Bloom

for Diana Bellessi

Abutilon: flowering indoor maple; houseplant

Cultivated inside   out of the bounds
of nature   it stubborned
on the windowsill   six winters and springs
resisting water   sun   all researched care.
It would not give   beyond its leaves.

Yet today   in the morning light
the sudden color asserts itself
among the spotted green   and I
pause   before another empty day
and wonder at its wild blooming.

It leans against the sunwarm glass
its blossoms firm on the thick stems
as if its roots
absorbed the knowledge
that there is no other place
that memory is only pain
that even here   now
we must burst forth with orange flowers
with savage hues of our captivity.

IV. Inhospitable Soil

i can't go back
where i came from was
burned off the map

i'm a jew
anywhere is someone else's land

—Melanie Kaye

Glimpses of the Outside

in memory of
Marcia Tillotson (1940-1981)

A place

1.

Cherry Plain was once called South Berlin   before
the war   and then they probably became self-conscious.
Many here   go back before the Revolution   are of
Hessian descent   fought with the British. They are
wary of strangers   defined as anyone who has not lived
here since birth. Still they chat politely   wave
as I drive by. The children are more open   stare
shamelessly   at the new woman in town. It is a quiet
place. One post office. One small general store.
It could have grown and developed   when they expanded
old route 22. But it would have meant   cutting into
the cemetery   and of course   that was out of the question.
Like disgruntled children   they protest over their parents'
limitations   for they see   they could have gotten something
off the weekenders   rushing back and forth on Friday
and Sunday nights. But ancestors will have their way.
So 22 looped around it   leaving the town intact   except
for the occasional stranger   who is looking for a way out.

2.

I have decided not to plant a garden   only to scavenge.
Already last year's furrows   (the result of others'
labor)   are vague   and the borders almost completely
obscured by the undisciplined   self-absorbed growth.
It is what we know of weeds: no delicate sense of
intrusion   of transgressing bounds. They move in
take over   and that's that. It doesn't bother me
this unreflecting rudeness. I am satisfied to witness
the few carrot sprigs   onions   tiny lettuce heads
and without commitment   to clear weedless islands
around them. The asparagus reaches its full growth

61

merges with the stalk   and goes to seed. The delicate
dill   follows suit   achieves its natural toughness.
I do not intercede   in these events.

3.

This house was once a meeting hall   then a dance
hall   a polling place. More recently   a garage.
I want to plant flowers around its edges   bring
to life an image   I have had about it. But the
earth is naturally tough with rocks   and more   it
is clogged with rusted screws and washers   sparkplugs
colored chips of glass   all conspiring against my
trowel. Then too there is the heavy oil   already
congealed   fixed and unyielding   like ancient geological
strata. The inner image long forgotten   I tense
against this human resistance   push harder towards
an earlier time   towards less polluted soil.

4.

I have started transplanting wild flowers   whose
names I do not know. Small blue ones from a lake
in a state park. They are modest   with pale yellow
centers   used to the moisture of the water's edge.
I douse them every morning to make them feel at home.
From a roadside   I dig out bright yellow ones   plant
them by the unpainted barn   so I can see them from my
window as I work. These thrive   as if their sole pur-
pose   was my pleasure. But exotic   tall purple flowers
with bulb-type roots   strong like twine in their tie
to the earth   and to their particular spot   these shrivel
up a few hours after being placed by the barn. I consider
the possibilities: individual will   personality   simple
biochemical make-up. Whatever. These do not adapt.
They stand tall   and elegant   dried by the sun   next to
the brilliant yellow flowers   for whom a place by the barn
is as good   as a roadbank.

5.

Midnight: the meadow is sparkling with fireflies.
I had always thought   that at night   they folded their
wings   over their iridescent bodies   and darkened
that light. Yet here they are   in constant motion
lighting against the shadow of the mountain. The
memory suddenly comes alive   like the underside of
a non-living stone. I am eight years old   and it is
almost dusk. The fireflies rush   through arid city
air. I trap them in a milk bottle   hoping to create
a lantern to light my way home. I do not understand
that not even the dusty grass   hurriedly pressed through
the narrow bottleneck   will keep them alive   that
inevitably   in such confinement (is it a lack of air
or simply a lack of space for flight?)   their light will
dim and die.

6.

What could go wrong in such a setting? I ask
myself   thinking of that arid air   left behind
of the wino sleeping in my doorway   every night.
This valley   is so quiet   so clear and sharp-
edged   in the summer daylight. The old houses
meticulously painted   and the lawns carefully mowed
declare only: order and plain living. What could
go wrong in such a setting? I ask myself again.
The mountains look permanent   eternal in fact
though all I read about human life   about natural
evolution   tells me everything is in constant
motion   that this landscape was once of a different
sort   that these people who distrust strangers
were once strangers themselves   that the sign
"Indian Massacre Road"   a sign indistinguishable
from any other in lettering and color   posted modestly
at an obscure crossing   is but a barely noticeable
vestige   of one history forgotten and unattended.

7.

The pump is old   its age reflected in its weight
iron   shaped and welded more than a half a century ago.
It draws the water noisily   slowly   sounding like
a failing heart   pounding against itself. The plumbers
cluck their tongues   in masculine admiration. "She's
a goddam antique"   the young one says. He is tall
and handsome   with clear blue eyes. "Don't make those
anymore"   he continues   with a voice of experience
his age denies. I suspect he's only an apprentice   for
he descends into the well   while the older man sits
casually on the ledge   occasionally offering advice.
They're in agreement   or in cahoots. Get a new pump.
This one's definitely shot. Not worth fixing   the parts
too difficult to find   and when found   too expensive.
I decide against it   at least for now   and tell them
to see if anything can be done. Later   I return and
ask   if they can patch it up. "Sure"   the young one
answers. "I'll take anything on   as long as it's white."

A visit

1.

The woman who is coming to visit   is my mother.
Her life   has been bracketed by historical events
over which she's had no control. During World War II
she developed a canniness for detecting Jews   did
not care how many documents they had to prove   who
they were not. She knew. She could tell   by a special
look in their eyes   a gesture of the hand   a confidence
too casual. This acquired ability   so finely tuned
during the war years   remains alive   so that today
decades later   she cannot wander far from her Jewish
neighborhood   before she begins assessing   who are
the safe ones   and who are not.

2.

Her survival   (and as a result mine)   was partly
dependent on: her small nose   her grey eyes. And
most critical: her impeccable Polish   (with no trace
of a Yiddish accent)   because an older sister had
insisted she attend Polish schools   to gain greater
mobility. It was one perspective on the Jewish condition
in Poland. At critical moments   these elements   heredity
and environment   combined in the right proportions to
create luck. But there was also another   character
or in this case   guts. When the Germans came for her
she begged: *Ich habe ein kleines kind.* And when she
saw   the sliver of hesitation in their eyes   she ran
and took her chances. They did not chase   or shoot
just let her go. For months   she convinced the peasants
she was a Pole   playing a part   ad-libbing the dialogue
without a flaw   pretending to be the human being   they
assumed she was. During this time   she learned survival
depends on complete distrust. Even today   she is still
fierce   in her refusal to rely on others. Some would call
it alienation. Others pride. I think   it's only
the necessary stance   of any survivor.

3.

History   she says with irony   has a way of repeating
itself. *Then*   she outwitted two German soldiers   probably
young men   taught from childhood   the hideousness of
Jews. Faced with a woman   fair and ordinary   pleading
for her sickly child who would be orphaned   they must have
thought: No   this cannot be that Jewish monster. And
she escaped. At least momentarily. *Now*   she is trapped
again. But no walls or barbed wire   around her this time.
No plans for uprisings   or secret meetings. Each evening
she returns   hurrying through the orderly streets   ominous
in their emptiness   and steps into the elevator. I want
to offer her advice   strategy   a philosophy   but know their
utter uselessness in this age. For *now*   is a vastly
different time and place. The country is not occupied
by strangers. Those she fears most   are not an enemy.
And neglect and hunger   cannot be outwitted.

4.

We visit the Hancock Shaker Village   walking through
the restored buildings   recreated workrooms and living
quarters. I note the quietness   the simplicity of
the line   and wonder about the eye that fashioned it
the aesthetic vision   the philosophy of light   air
of raising the struggle for survival   above humiliation.
We pass through the herb garden. My mother stops
looks in amazement at the round stone barn   and marvels
how all this could have come   to a dead stop   without
catastrophe   without disaster. She scrutinizes the
photographs of children   adopted and nurtured. "How
could they not have wanted children of their own?"
she asks   having always believed   that one's own blood is
the sole source   of all security. And I see her shift
as she tells me again   of the children   hidden in convents
baptised and converted   then claimed by relatives after
the war. Many were finally kidnapped   or their protectors
bribed and bought off. Some could never be reclaimed.
For those who were   it was hard   painful   but my mother
adds   "They were our only hope."

5.

But it is not simply a question of reproduction
I tell myself that night   thinking of my own child-
lessness. They lacked something   which would have
pushed them on   which would have given them   a hook
in time. But it was time itself   that they ignored
thinking the farmland and woods   around the village
the seasons emerging predictably   in full character
the day and the night   all these   they assumed were
heaven   eternal. At the end of each day   after baking
and laundry   welding and weaving   tending the children
and the fields   they would meet   and reaffirm their faith.
First they shook out the sins from their bodies   then
danced holding their palms up   to gather in the blessings.
There was no time   there was no death. And so they
lived   and so they died.

6.

My mother boards the train   and sits behind the
tinted glass. She mouths words and gestures   nothing
I can understand. I raise my arms in frustration
motion her to try again. She does   but the barriers
remain. She writes a note   on a piece of paper   holds
it against the glass. The European script is clear:
"It is empty here. It is cool." I smile   and give
the okay sign. She will be comfortable on her trip back
to the city. Still   I am all anxiety. Departures
swell old   undefined fears in me   the fear of permanent
separations. Old   long-forgotten departures   which
remain active in me   like instinct. The fear of being
lost and never found   of losing all trace   all connections
severed   the thread broken. (When after two years   she
came to get me from the orphanage   I cried when I caught
sight of her   and raised my arms to her. I was barely
three   but I had not forgotten.) Of endless   futile
searches for relatives long vanished   or even worse
alive   but not traceable.

The train begins to move. My mother sits behind the tinted glass and waves. Her face becomes an angle   and then disappears. Her words were: "Find a place where you are happy." But the sound of those words   had the mourning of separation.

A place in time

1.

The postmistress is insecure in her calculations.
She checks   and rechecks all her figures   never having
the ease of certainty. Still   I trust her view
of this place   for she has that tutored eye   able to
detect the changes   nuances and variations   whose
implications   remain obscure to my alien reasoning.
She is chatty   inquisitive. Sometimes   I think she must
be lonely   sitting all day by herself   behind the old-
fashioned post office boxes   decorated with elaborate
brass eagles. Perhaps the grocery will be sold (and then
we'll be stuck   with whoever buys it). Perhaps the mail
truck   will be traded in   (and then we'll have regular
delivery). Perhaps the church will be painted   by early
fall (and we can begin having services again). Perhaps
the rumors about the metal barrels   buried in the nearby
camp grounds are true   (and we should stop swimming
in that lake).

2.

At first   the cats were cautious   flattening
themselves   along the ground   slinking close to
the edges of the house. No vestigial recollections
springing from the unconscious depth of the species.
Or so I thought. But now   and I can hardly measure
the time elapsed   they act as if it's all they've
ever known   routinely bringing in mice from the meadow
or bodies of birds   necks snapped   heads hanging
like colored limp sacks. I glimpse my favorite
the tortoise shell   eating a rabbit   whose belly seems
expertly slashed and exposed. She hunches   over it
calmly chewing   the juicy red meat   patiently breaking
through   the sinewy flesh.

69

3.

At the Burr & Grille in Averill Park   only men
are at the bar. They look like mechanics: oil
streaked pants   workgloves stuffed in pockets.
They swap army stories   their glimpses of the
outside. In Haiti   I overhear   there are only
the rich and the poor. "Nothing in the middle"
a man in his twenties says. The rich live on top
of the mountain   the poor by the sea. They earn
about $35 a year. "Imagine the kind of life   *that*
is. They're starving. Imagine! In this day and age!"
Burr   behind the bar   clucks his tongue. "In China"
he says   "they fight over candybars. Imagine what
that must be like." The young one begins again:
"You know   you get off   and they have all those
bands and colorful costumes   and everything is all
welcome. And then you take five steps away from
the pier   and *wham!* [he bangs his hand down on the bar]
they're ready to slit your throat   to get that wallet!"

4.

Saturday: The Baptist Church flea market and auction
offers the predictable merchandise. Old clothes
battered pots and pans   chipped glassware   rusted lawn
furniture. "It's all for a good cause"   a woman tells
me   and mentions interior renovations. I wonder if I'm
the only Jew in the crowd. An older man approaches.
"Smile!" he orders. "The Lord loves you! Certainly
the Lord loves you!" I nod   feel uncomfortable   move
towards another table. A woman   about seven months
pregnant   is having her purchases priced. She is no
more than twenty   with a small pale face   faintly freckled
deeply worn. Dressed in colorless bermudas   and a gray
blouse   she holds a carton of baby clothes. On the ground
by her feet are cheap games of plastic   a round container
with broken wooden logs   the debris of an old erector set.
This too   is her collection   the necessary response
to life's gnawing insistence on itself   on not being

ignored. She looks wearied   almost emptied by her vigilance.
I watch as she hands over the ten dollar bill and waits
for the change   watch   as she smiles   and turns away.

5.

I ride the backroads   far from any village or town
far from the blacktops   carefully numbered. Woods
along both sides. Suddenly   I am startled by an
unexpected home   a trailer on a small patch of cleared
land. Logic would say   that it had no stability
the cinderblocks at its corners appearing flimsy   unable
to keep it firmly rooted to the ground. Yet the faded
paint   the obvious rust creeping along its outer shell
reveal a hard-won permanence. Barefoot children stop
playing in front of a torn screen door   stand anxious
tentative   waiting for the unfamiliar car to pass.
A woman's eyes   keep guard at a kitchen window. Plastic
deer and clay ducks line the worn path. Junked cars
spill out of the collapsed garage. Gray overalls   and
bright sheets with sunsets   dry between two shade trees.
In a carved out tractor tire   painted red and white   grow
yellow marigolds   blue petunias. An orderly vegetable
garden on one side   loose piles of freshly split logs
on the other   testify to the implacable needs of winter.
All is urgency   asymmetry in this territory resistant
to maps and philosophy. Only the seasons   and birth
and death   remain stark. I know   I see   I learn again
from the anxiety in that woman's eyes   in the caution
of the children's stance   that there is no escape.

Mourning

1.

I reread his letter. He writes about your struggle
Marcia   your will to survive. I read the letter again
and stare at the mountain's outline   behind the house.
It is will   against the dark shadowy mountain   that I
keep thinking about. How you refused   up to the last
moment   refused to say   it is over   but stretched out
your time   how you were willing to endure the pain   how
you would not be separated from it   because it alone
held the possibility of life. A few days before you died
a friend said: *Everything's collapsing   but she simply
refuses.* I think about that refusal to cooperate   to give
yourself an easeful death. It is your will   Marcia
I am trying to understand.

2.

Why so hard to absorb   after all the waiting?
The daily calls   and reports   turned your body
into a machine. The nurses were polite   precise.
Respiratory arrest. Cardiac failure. She's
breathing on her own now. Somewhat better.
"How is her spirit?" I ask stupidly   as if
the answer could make a bond between us. One
time they said: She is angry.   Another: She is
somewhat anxious.

3.

Death asserts itself as everywhere   pulls me out
of the eternal   roots me in this time   in this place.
Your death   Marcia. After thirteen years of struggles
who would have thought   this was the final one   who
would have thought   this one was different   from all
the others? It is something I must plant   I keep saying
as if I could contain the loss   by finding the right
piece of ground   by the barn perhaps   or by the gigantic

ash   that hovers over the house   a tree planted by
a neighbor's father   more than sixty years ago. I
need a place for your death   Marcia   for it feels like
an emptiness   that can erode   all the mountains
that protect this valley.

4.

But there is no possibility of containing it. All
the days merge   and only hindsight   reveals the subtle
but discrete changes: the shortened daylight
the slowly   yellowing grass. I place seeds in the bird
feeder   write letters home   check the final stages of
the garden's undisciplined growth. Everything is
shrivelling   emptying itself of body and substance
huddling closer and closer to the earth. I plant bulbs
like a skeptic   never fully believing   these drab
lifeless lumps   will bloom next year   in full exotic color.
Nothing   I think   staring at the sixty-year-old ash
should be taken for granted. I push my trowel   deeper
sift out the slivers of glass   the heavy nails   place
the bulbs in their designated places   then cover them
with soil   flattening the surface with my hand.

Bashert

These words are dedicated to those who died

These words are dedicated to those who died
because they had no love and felt alone in the world
because they were afraid to be alone and tried to stick it out
because they could not ask
because they were shunned
because they were sick and their bodies could not resist the
disease
because they played it safe
because they had no connections
because they had no faith
because they felt they did not belong and wanted to die

These words are dedicated to those who died
because they were loners and liked it
because they acquired friends and drew others to them
because they took risks
because they were stubborn and refused to give up
because they asked for too much

These words are dedicated to those who died
because a card was lost and a number was skipped
because a bed was denied
because a place was filled and no other place was left

These words are dedicated to those who died
because someone did not follow through
because someone was overworked and forgot
because someone left everything to God
because someone was late
because someone did not arrive at all
because someone told them to wait and they just couldn't any
longer

These words are dedicated to those who died
because death is a punishment
because death is a reward

ba-shert (Yiddish): inevitable, (pre)destined.

74

because death is the final rest
because death is eternal rage

These words are dedicated to those who died

Bashert

These words are dedicated to those who survived

These words are dedicated to those who survived
because their second grade teacher gave them books
because they did not draw attention to themselves and got lost
in the shuffle
because they knew someone who knew someone else who could
help them and bumped into them on a corner on a Thursday
afternoon
because they played it safe
because they were lucky

These words are dedicated to those who survived
because they knew how to cut corners
because they drew attention to themselves and always got picked
because they took risks
because they had no principles and were hard

These words are dedicated to those who survived
because they refused to give up and defied statistics
because they had faith and trusted in God
because they expected the worst and were always prepared
because they were angry
because they could ask
because they mooched off others and saved their strength
because they endured humiliation
because they turned the other cheek
because they looked the other way

These words are dedicated to those who survived
because life is a wilderness and they were savage
because life is an awakening and they were alert
because life is a flowering and they blossomed
because life is a struggle and they struggled
because life is a gift and they were free to accept it

These words are dedicated to those who survived

Bashert

1. Poland, 1944: My mother is walking down a road.

My mother is walking down a road. Somewhere in Poland. Walking towards an unnamed town for some kind of permit. She is carrying her Aryan identity papers. She has left me with an old peasant who is willing to say she is my grandmother.

She is walking down a road. Her terror in leaving me behind, in risking the separation is swallowed now, like all other feelings. But as she walks, she pictures me waving from the dusty yard, imagines herself suddenly picked up, the identity papers challenged. And even if she were to survive that, would she ever find me later? She tastes the terror in her mouth again. She swallows.

I am over three years old, corn silk blond and blue eyed like any Polish child. There is terrible suffering among the peasants. Starvation. And like so many others, I am ill. Perhaps dying. I have bad lungs. Fever. An ugly ear infection that oozes pus. None of these symptoms are disappearing.

The night before, my mother feeds me watery soup and then sits and listens while I say my prayers to the Holy Mother, Mother of God. I ask her, just as the nuns taught me, to help us all: me, my mother, the old woman. And then catching myself, learning to use memory, I ask the Mother of God to help my father. The Polish words slip easily from my lips. My mother is satisfied. The peasant has perhaps heard and is reassured. My mother has found her to be kind, but knows that she is suspicious of strangers.

My mother is sick. Goiter. Malnutrition. Vitamin deficiencies. She has skin sores which she cannot cure. For months now she has been living in complete isolation, with no point of reference outside of herself. She has been her own sole advisor, companion, comforter. Almost everyone of her world is dead: three sisters, nephews and nieces, her mother, her husband, her in-laws. All gone. Even the remnants of the resistance, those few left after the uprising, have dispersed into the Polish countryside. She is more alone than she could have ever imagined. Only she knows her real name and she is perhaps dying. She is thirty years old.

I am over three years old. I have no consciousness of our danger, our separateness from the others. I have no awareness that we are playing a part. I only know that I have a special name, that I have been named for the Goddess of Peace. And each night, I sleep secure in that knowledge. And when I wet my bed, my mother places me on her belly and lies on the stain. She fears the old woman and hopes her body's warmth will dry the sheet before dawn.

My mother is walking down a road. Another woman joins her. My mother sees through the deception, but she has promised herself that never, under any circumstances, will she take that risk. So she swallows her hunger for contact and trust and instead talks about the sick child left behind and lies about the husband in the labor camp.

Someone is walking towards them. A large, strange woman with wild red hair. They try not to look at her too closely, to seem overly curious. But as they pass her, my mother feels something move inside her. The movement grows and grows till it is an explosion of yearning that she cannot contain. She stops, orders her companion to continue without her. And then she turns.

The woman with the red hair has also stopped and turned. She is grotesque, bloated with hunger, almost savage in her rags. She and my mother move towards each other. Cautiously, deliberately, they probe past the hunger, the swollen flesh, the infected skin, the rags. Slowly, they begin to pierce five years of encrusted history. And slowly, there is perception and recognition.

In this wilderness of occupied Poland, in this vast emptiness where no one can be trusted, my mother has suddenly, bizarrely, met one of my father's teachers. A family friend. Another Jew.

They do not cry, but weep as they chronicle the dead and count the living. Then they rush to me. To the woman I am a familiar sight. She calculates that I will not live out the week, but comments only on my striking resemblance to my father. She says she has contacts. She leaves. One night a package of food is delivered anonymously. We eat. We begin to bridge the gap towards life. We survive.

2. Chicago, 1964: I am walking home alone at midnight.

I am walking home alone at midnight. I am a student of literature, and each night I stay in the library until it closes. Yet each night, as I return I still feel unprepared for the next day. The nature of literary movements eludes me. I only understand individual writers. I have trouble remembering genre definitions, historical dates and names, cannot grasp their meaning, significance. A whole world of abstractions and theories remains beyond my reach, on the other side of a wall I cannot climb over.

So each night, I walk home clutching my books as if I were a small school child. The city is alien. Since coming to America, this is my first time away from a Jewish neighborhood, Jewish friends, and I feel isolated, baffled at how to make a place for myself in this larger, gentile world which I have entered.

I am walking home alone at midnight. The university seems an island ungrounded. Most of its surrounding streets have been emptied. On some, all evidence of previous life removed except for occasional fringes of rubble that reveal vague outlines that hint at things that were. On others, old buildings still stand, though these are hollow like caves, once of use and then abandoned. Everything is poised. Everything is waiting for the emptiness to close in upon itself, for the emptiness to be filled up, for the emptiness to be swallowed and forgotten.

Walking home, I am only dimly aware of the meaning of this strange void through which I pass. I am even less aware of the dangers for someone like me, a woman walking home alone at midnight. I am totally preoccupied with another time, another place. Night after night, protected by the darkness, I think only of Elza who is dead. I am trying to place a fact about her, a fact which stubbornly resists classification: nothing that happened to her afterwards mattered. All that agonized effort. All that caring. *None of that mattered!*

At the end of the war, friends come to claim her. With the cold, calculated cunning of an adult, the eight year old vehemently denies who she is. No she is not who they think. Not a Jew. They have made a mistake. Mixed her up with another Elza. This one belongs here, with her mother.

79

She is simply being scrupulous in following her parents' instructions. "Do not ever admit to anyone who you are. It is our secret. Eventually we will come for you. Remember! *Never admit who you are!* Promise!"

Four years later, the war is over. Her parents dead. She is still bound by her promise. This woman *is* her mother. Her parents' friends know better. The woman has been kind, has saved her. But she is a Pole and Elza is a Jew. Finally, the bribe is big enough and the child released. Elza becomes an orphan.

And afterwards? She is adopted and finally seems to have everything. Two parents. Two handsome brothers. A house. Her own room. She studies Latin and does translations. Is valedictorian of her class. Goes away to college. Has boyfriends, affairs. Comes to New York. Works. Begins graduate school. Explicates Dylan Thomas, T. S. Eliot. Marries.

But none of it matters. She cannot keep up. The signs are clear. She is a poor housekeeper. Insists they eat off paper plates. She buys enough clothes to fill all her closets. But nothing soothes her. Finally she signs her own papers. Is released within a few months. I finish college and leave for Europe. Three weeks later, she checks into a hotel and takes an overdose. She is twenty-five years old.

Fearing I too might be in danger, my mother instructs Polish Jews resettled in Paris and Tel Aviv: "Don't tell her!" And to me she writes: "Elza is in the hospital again. There is no hope." I am suspicious, refer to her whenever I can. I am alert. Sense a discomfort, an edge I cannot define. I think I know, but I never dare ask. I come home. Seven months after her death, I finally know.

A story she once told me remains alive. During the war, the Polish woman sends her to buy a notebook for school. She is given the wrong change and points it out. The shopkeeper eyes her sharply: "Very accurate. Just like a Jew. Perhaps you are a little Jewess?" And Elza feels afraid and wonders if this woman sees the truth in her blue eyes.

Another memory. Elza is reading accounts of the war. She cannot help herself she tells me. An anecdote explains something to her. A woman in a camp requests a bandage for a wound. And the guard, so startled by her simplicity and directness, makes sure she gets one. That woman, Elza tells me, refused to stop acting like a human being. Jews, she concludes, made a terrible mistake.

I am walking home alone at midnight. I am raw with the pain of her death. I wonder. Is it inevitable? Everything that happened to us afterwards, to all of us, does none of it matter? Does it not matter what we do and where we live? Are there moments in history which cannot be escaped or transcended, but which act like time warps permanently trapping all those who are touched by them? And that which should have happened in 1944 in Poland and didn't, must it happen now? In 1964? In Chicago? Or can history be tricked and cheated?

These questions haunt me. Yet I persist with a will I myself do not understand. I continue reading, studying, making friends. And as the rawness of Elza's death eases and becomes familiar, as time becomes distance, I find myself more and more grounded in my present life, in my passion for words and literature. I begin to perceive the world around me. I develop perspective.

I see the rubble of this unbombed landscape, see that the city, like the rest of this alien country, is not simply a geographic place, but a time zone, an era in which I, by my very presence in it, am rooted. No one simply passes through. History keeps unfolding and demanding a response. A life obliterated around me of those I barely noticed. A life unmarked, unrecorded. A silent mass migration. Relocation. Common rubble in the streets.

I see now the present dangers, the dangers of the void, of the American hollowness in which I walk calmly day and night as I continue my life. I begin to see the incessant grinding down of lines for stamps, for jobs, for a bed to sleep in, of a death stretched imperceptibly over a lifetime. I begin to understand the ingenuity of it. The invisibility. The Holocaust without smoke.

Everything is poised. Everything is waiting for the emptiness to be filled up, for the filling-up that can never replace, that can only take over. Like time itself. Or history.

3. Brooklyn, 1971: I am almost equidistant from two continents.

I am almost equidistant from two continents. I look back towards one, then forward towards the other. The moment is approaching when I will be equidistant from both and will have to choose. Maintaining equidistance is not a choice.

By one of those minor and peculiar coincidences that permanently shape and give texture to our lives, I am born on my father's twenty-eighth birthday. Two years later, exactly three days after his thirtieth and my second birthday, he is dead in the brush factory district of the Warsaw Ghetto. His corpse is buried in a courtyard and eventually the spot blends with the rest of the rubble. The Uprising, my birth, his death—all merge and become interchangeable. That is the heritage of one continent.

In one of the classes that I teach, all the students are Black and Puerto Rican. I am the only white. Initially, the students are nervous, wondering if I will be a hard task master. I am nervous too, though I do not yet have a name for it. After a few months together, we grow accustomed to each other. I am trying to understand my role here. That is the heritage of the other continent.

And now, approaching my own thirtieth birthday, approaching the moment when I will be equidistant from the two land masses, I feel some kind of cellular breakdown in my body, a sudden surging inside me, as if flesh and muscle and bone were losing definition. Everything in me yearns to become transparent, to be everywhere, to become like the water between two vast land masses that will never touch. I desire to become salt water, to establish the connection.

I am almost equidistant from two continents.

April 17, 1955. I have been asked to light one of the six candles. I stand on the stage in the large, darkened auditorium, wait to be called, wait to accept the flame, to pass it on like a memory. I am numb with terror at the spectacle around me. I fear these people with blue numbers on their arms, people who are disfigured and scarred, who have missing limbs and uneasy walks, people whose histories repel me. Here in this auditorium, they abandon all inhibitions, they transform themselves into pure sound, the sound of irretrievable loss, of wild pain and sorrow. Then they become all flesh, wringing their hands and covering their swollen eyes and flushed faces. They call out to me and I feel myself dissolving.

When it is time for me to come forward, to light the candle for those children who were burned, who were shot, who were stomped to death, I move without feeling. And as I near the candelabra, I hear them call out the common Yiddish names: *Surele. Moyshele. Channele. Rivkele. Yankele. Shayndele. Rayzl. Benyomin. Chavele. Miriam. Chaim.* The names brush against my face, invade my ears, my mouth. I breathe them into my lungs, into my bones. And as the list continues, guided by their sounds, I cross the stage and light the sixth and final candle. It is my fourteenth birthday.

I am almost equidistant from two continents.

March, 1971. There are twenty-eight people in the class. Eighteen women, ten men. Some married. Some single. Alone. With children. With parents and grandparents. Nieces. Nephews. They are here because they have not met the minimum standards of this college. This class is their special chance to catch up. Subject and verb agreement. Sentence fragments. Pronoun reference. Vocabulary building. Paragraph organization. Topic sentence. Reading comprehension. Study skills. Discipline. All this to catch up, or as one student said to me, his eyes earnest: "I want to write so that when I go for a job they won't think I'm lazy."

I am required to take attendance. I check through the names, call them out each morning: *James. Reggie. Marie. Simone. Joy. Christine. Alvarez. Ashcroft. Basile. Colon. Corbett. White. Raphael. Dennis. Juan. Carissa. Lamont. Andrea.* Fragments of their lives fall before me. The chaos and disorganization. A mother needing help in filling out forms in English. A sick child. Hospital regulations. A brother looking for a job. Another brother in trouble. Welfare red tape. Unemployment payment restrictions. Waiting lists. Eviction. SRO. The daily grind interrupting their catching-up, and the increasing sense that with each day missed, they fall further behind.

I am almost equidistant from two continents. I look back towards one, then forward towards the other. There is a need in me to become transparent like water, to become the salt water which is their only connection.

March, 1971. Marie wants to study medicine. She concedes it's a long haul, but, as she says, "It's only time. What difference does it make?" Slightly older than the others, she lives alone with her daughter. To some of the women's horror, she refuses to have a telephone, does not like to be intruded upon. When necessary, she can always be reached through a neighbor. She rarely misses class, on a few occasions brings her daughter with her who sits serenely drawing pictures. Facing Marie, I sometimes do not know who I am and wonder how she perceives me. She seems oblivious to my discomfort. She is only focused on the class, always reworking her assignments, reading everything twice, asking endless questions to make sure she really understands. One day, at the end of the hour, when we are alone, she asks: "What are you?" I am caught off guard, know the meaning of the question, but feel the resistance in me. I break it down and answer quietly: "A Jew." She nods and in that moment two vast land masses touch.

Each continent has its legacy. The day I reach my thirtieth birthday, the age of my father's death, I am equidistant from both. And as the moment passes, everything in me becomes defined again. I am once again muscle, flesh, bone. America is not my chosen home, not even the place of my birth. Just a spot where it seemed safe to go to escape certain dangers. But safety, I discover, is only temporary. No place guarantees it to anyone forever. I have stayed because there is no other place to go. In my muscles, my flesh, my bone, I balance the heritages, the histories of two continents.

4. Cherry Plain, 1981: I have become a keeper of accounts.

There are moments when I suddenly become breathless, as if I had just tricked someone, but was afraid the ruse would be exposed and I'd be hunted again. At those moments, the myths that propel our history, that turn fiction into fact, emerge in full force in me, as I stare into the eyes of strangers or someone suddenly grown alien. And when I see their eyes become pinpoints of judgments, become cold and indifferent, or simply distanced with curiousity, at those moments I hear again the words of the Polish woman:

Very accurate. Just like a Jew. You are perhaps a little Jewess?

At moments such as these I teeter, shed the present, and like rage, like pride, like acceptance, like the refusal to deny, I call upon the ancient myths again and say:

Yes. It's true. All true. I am scrupulously accurate. I keep track of all distinctions. Between past and present. Pain and pleasure. Living and surviving. Resistance and capitulation. Will and circumstances. Between life and death. Yes. I am scrupulously accurate. I have become a keeper of accounts.

Like the patriarchs, the shabby scholars who only lived for what was written and studied it all their lives

Like the inhuman usurers and dusty pawnbrokers who were quarantined within precisely prescribed limits of every European town and who were as accurate as the magistrates that drew the boundaries of their lives and declared them diseased

Like those men of stone who insisted that the *goyim* fulfil the contracts they had signed and who responded to the tearful pleas of illness, weakness, sudden calamity and poverty, with the words: "What are these to me? You have made me a keeper of accounts. Give me my pound of flesh. It says on this piece of paper, you owe me a pound of flesh!"

Like those old, heartless, dried up merchants whose entire lives were spent in the grubby *shtetl* streets that are now but memory, whose only body softness was in their fingertips worn smooth by silver coins, whose vision that all that mattered was on pieces of paper was proven absolutely accurate, when their

złoty, francs, and marks could not buy off the written words
Żyd, Juif, Jude

Like these, my despised ancestors
I have become a keeper of accounts.

And like all the matriarchs, the wives and daughters, the sisters
and aunts, the nieces, the keepers of button shops, milliners,
seamstresses, peddlers of foul fish, of matches, of rotten apples,
laundresses, midwives, floor washers and street cleaners, who
rushed exhausted all week so that *shabes* could be observed
with fresh *challah* on the table, who argued in the common
tongue

and begged for the daughter run off to the revolution
and the daughter run off with a *shegetz*
who refused to sit *shiva* and say *kaddish* for a living child
who always begged for life
who understood the accounts but saw them differently
who knew the power of human laws, knew they always counted
no matter what the revolution or the party or the state
who knew the power of the words *Żyd, Juif, Jude*

who cried whole lifetimes for their runaway children
for the husbands immobilized by the written word
for the brother grown callous from usury
for the uncle grown indifferent from crime, from bargaining,
from chiseling, from jewing them down

Like these, my despised ancestors
I have become a keeper of accounts.

I do not shun this legacy. I claim it as mine   whenever I see
the photographs of nameless people. Standing staring off the
edge of the picture. People dressed in coats lined with fur. Or
ragged at elbows and collar. Hats cocked on one side glancing
anxiously toward the lens. A peasant cap centered and ordinary.
Hair styled in the latest fashion. Or standing ashamed a coarse
wig awkwardly fitted. The shabby clothes. Buttons missing. The
elegant stance. Diamond rings. Gold teeth. The hair being
shaved. The face of humiliation. The hand holding the child's
hand. A tree. A track. A vague building in a photograph. A fa-

cility. And then the fields of hair   the endless fields of hair
the earth growing fertile with their bodies   with their souls.

Old   rarely seen types. Gone   they say   forever. And yet I
know they can be revived again   that I can trigger them again.
That they awaken in me   for I have felt it happen   in the
sight of strangers   or someone suddenly grown alien. When-
ever I have seen the judgment   the coldness   and indiffer-
ence   the distanced curiousity.   At those moments   I
teeter   shed my present self   and all time merges   and
like rage   like pride   like acceptance   like the refusal to
deny   I answer

Yes. It is true.   I am a keeper of accounts.

Bashert

Solitary Acts

for my aunt
Gina Klepfisz (1908?-1942)

"To garden is a solitary act."
                              —Michelle Cliff

1.

And to die
as you did   with the father
confessor   standing   waiting
patiently   for your death
for your final words
and you   watching the dissolution
around you   watching his eyes
his face   listening to his Latin words
said: "What have I to confess?
I am a Jew."

It was 1942   and you wanted someone
to know   though you'd be buried
in a Christian grave   with an Aryan name.

Such will to be known   can alter history.

2.

Today   I stand alone   planning my first garden
and think of you   buried on that other continent
rescued from the Christian plot
the only flesh of your family   to lie
in a marked grave   in the Jewish cemetery
in a Warsaw   almost empty of any Jews.
That ground   I know   is but a fragment
of the past   a place apart   the surroundings
long rebuilt   into a modern city
and I know   that even now
while I stand   and try to map this season's growth
that country   cleansed of our people's blood
intones the litany of old complaints.

Gina   they hate us still.

3.

You are to me   everything
that remains   outside my grasp
everything   in this world
that is destroyed   with no one
there to rescue the fragments
to hear the words.
So much of history   seems
a gaping absence   at best a shadow
longing   for some greater
definition   which will never come
for what is burned   becomes air
and ashes   nothing more.

So I cling   to the knowledge of your
distant grave   for it alone
reminds me   prods me   to shape that shadow.

4.

I have spent a life   disentangling from influences
trying to claim   what was original   mine:
from my mother's mastery   of daily survival
so subtly interwoven   with common gestures
few recognize it   for what it is
from my father's more visibly   heroic deed
of dying   recorded in memoirs   tributes
from the deaths of grandparents   aunts   uncles
anonymous   in a heap   indistinguishable
from all the others   who died unmourned.

And now   I remember you   and face another:
Gina   in those few months   when you watched
over me   before my consciousness learned
the danger   into which I had just been born
and the label   of who I was   and while my mother
sick and weak   teetered on the edge of life
in those few months   as the meaning of the ghetto
walls   grew more defined   as you inched people
out of the *umschlagplatz*   your chest contracting
gasping   with fear   yet certain that this needed to be done
I believe   that in that short time   something
passed between us   Gina   and you imparted to me
the vision   the firm sense of self   that gave
you strength   to state your name.

5.

And who would say   that I have mourned
enough   that I have looked at the old
photographs enough   yellowed and faded
and the green ink   now a grey dullness
where Marek   placed the flowers
on the rubble   where my father's body
was buried and disappeared   and Marek's head
looking down   his profile   etched against
an empty horizon   for there was nothing left

who would say   that I have mourned
enough?

And when I asked my mother if I
could have this album   that holds it all
holds more than most have   who are
without a witness   to mark their spot in green
or whose graves have been overgrown by weeds
or forests   or bulldozed for the sake
of modern cities   or whose bodies were never
buried   but were left for speechless animals
to devour   there is no piece of earth
that does not have its nameless   who lived
and died   unnoticed   beyond the grasp of history
who die today

And when I asked my mother   if I
could have this album   and she replied
this stays here   in this apartment
until I die   I glimpsed again the urgency
to be known.

6.

There have been many plots of ground
that formed me. This town's church
its cemetery   the bare   expectant earth
of my garden   all remind me   of that
other soil   on which I grew.

The first   was the green bush and grass
behind Marek's house in Lodz. It was
after the war   and Elza   orphaned   and just recently
claimed   from the Polish stranger   stood proud
before me   and brushed her long blond hair
her haughtiness   her only power. I watched
ashamed   and awkward   my small hand trying
to hide   my bald head   shaved for reasons
I was never told. It was our first meeting.

More than two years later   in the neutral
countryside that never saw the war   in Neglinge
Moti and I   crawled flat on our stomachs
to see the miniature wild flowers   hidden
beneath the blooming lilac bush. They grew
for elves   I said   and bound him to me
with the secret   not wanting anyone else
to know. He was alert then   but only months
before   had refused to eat   was force fed
in a Stockholm hospital. When his appetite
returned   he clung to me   four years older
in a way   no one could ever understand
and I responded   as I never would again
unconsciously   selflessly   with complete
certainty.   I knew that he must live
and inched him along.

And again   a few years later   in a park   the Bronx
there was an unmowed field   near a metal fence.
My mother would bring me here   on warm summer Sundays
and spread a blanket   that would billow
over the high   resistant grass   then finally settle
and flatten with the weight of our bodies.
We brought things to read   books that warmed

with the sun   newspapers   that yellowed
as the day wore on.

These were the gardens of my childhood.

7.

Gina   I must tell you: today I
felt hopeful   as I knelt close
to the earth   and turned it
inch by inch   sifting the soil
clearing the way   for roots
of vegetables. I felt so hopeful
Gina   that with repeated years
and efforts   the monotony of daily
motion   of bending   and someday
the earth   would be uncluttered
the debris cleared.

There is   I know   no reason
for such hope   for nothing destroyed
is ever made up   or restored to us.
In the earth   are buried histories
irretrievable.   Yet what philosophy
can justify   any of our emotions?
Like the watercolors from Buchenwald—
if you can imagine! The stench
from the chimneys   just the sounds
of the place. And yet someone felt
a need to paint. And did.

So do not ask me to explain
why I draw meaning and strength
from these common gestures   why today
my hope is unwavering   solid   as if
I'd never lost it   or never would again
as if those dying   angry or stunned
at the stupidity of it   could be revived
as if their mortal wounds   could heal
as if their hunger   could be outlived
as if they were not dying   strangers
to others   strangers to themselves.

I need to hope. And do.

8.

I have been a dreamer   dreaming
of a perfect garden   of a family tree
whose branches   spread   through centuries
of an orderly cemetery   with no gravestones
missing.   Tonight   as the sun sets   and I
turn towards evening   I have no such dreams.
Like the woman   who refused to trace
the ancient constellations   upon a clear
and crowded sky   because finding the stars
recording each in its place   the faint
and the brilliant   was enough
I too   Gina   have discarded all patterns
and blueprints. This night   I want only
to sleep   a dark   rich   dreamless sleep
to shelter   in me   what is left
to strengthen myself   for what is needed.

Cherry Plain, New York
August 1982

Notes

IV. Inhospitable Soil

"i can't go back. . . " from "Notes of an Immigrant Daughter: Atlanta" by Melanie Kaye in *Nice Jewish Girls: A Lesbian Anthology*, ed. Evelyn Torton Beck (Watertown, Massachusetts: Persephone Press Inc., 1982).

Glimpses of the Outside

Ich habe ein kleines kind. (German) I have a small child.

Bashert

goyim (Yiddish, pl.)—Gentiles

shtetl (Yiddish)—small-town Jewish community in Eastern Europe, where Yiddish culture flourished; these towns were completely destroyed by the end of World War II

złoty, francs, marks—Polish French, German monetary units

Żyd, Juif, Jude (Polish, French, German)—Jew

shabes (Yiddish)—Sabbath

challah (Yiddish)—a twisted white bread eaten on the Sabbath

shegetz (Yiddish)—Gentile man (pejorative)

shiva (Yiddish)—a seven-day mourning period for the dead

kaddish (Yiddish)—a prayer for the dead

Solitary Acts

"To garden is a solitary act." from "The Garden" in *Claiming an Identity They Taught Me to Despise* by Michelle Cliff (Watertown, Massachusetts: Persephone Press Inc., 1980).

umschlagplatz (German)—the place of deportation for concentration camps

"Like the watercolors from Buchenwald—" For the extraordinary artwork produced in ghettos, concentration camps and in hiding, see the reproductions in *The Art of the Holocaust*, eds. Janet Blatter and Sybil Milton (New York: Rutledge Press, 1981).

About the Author

Irena Klepfisz was born in Warsaw, Poland in 1941. She emigrated to the United States in 1949 and grew up in New York City. A graduate of the City College of New York, she received her Ph.D. in English from the University of Chicago. She has taught English, Yiddish, Women's Studies, and women's poetry workshops and has supported herself primarily as a secretary, copyeditor, proofreader, and typist. In 1975 she received a New York State CAPS grant in poetry, and in 1976 published her first collection, *periods of stress*. She was a founder and editor of *Conditions* magazine (1976-1981). Over the past six years her poetry, fiction and essays have appeared in numerous feminist and lesbian/feminist journals and anthologies. Her writings on anti-Semitism were recently included in *Nice Jewish Girls: A Lesbian Anthology* (Persephone Press).